Our Ancestors Are Proud

Written by:
Marvin Running River Banks

Cadmus Publishing
www.cadmuspublishing.com

Copyright © 2021 Marvin Running River Banks

Published by Cadmus Publishing
www.cadmuspublishing.com

ISBN: 978-1-63751-026-1

All rights reserved. Copyright under Berne Copyright Convention, Universal Copyright Convention, and Pan-American Copyright Convention. No part of this book may be reproduced, stored in a retrieval system, or transmitted in any form, or by any means, electronic, mechanical, photocopying, recording or otherwise, without prior permission of the author.

Dedications

This book is dedicated to the Ancestors and the next seven generations, which includes my daughter, Katrina Glodek.

I also dedicate this book to the late Dennis Banks and the American Indian Movement. To my teachers, Chief Good Bear (Ammon Bailey) Lakota, Ms. Jennifer Hudson and Mark Castles.

My grandmother. My Fellow Red Roaders: Brazil, Sleepy Rabbit, Steve Rozniakowski, a.k.a. Mad Dog, and the research his mom did for me early on, Young Wolf and Laughing Fox, and Jamon "Red Tail" Walker for being brave warriors standing alongside me against the racism of this prison.

My old heads Raven and Rambo and Maku, a.k.a. Rainbow Dancer," ex-slave name Mr. Pritchett LOL. Also, psychologist Ms. Mowry, Ms. Lane, Ms. Dunn, C.O. Gearhart, Sgt. Koone and C.O. Moore, a.k.a. Big Frog, I told you so.

Last, but not least, my manager and support through this whole ordeal, Jesse Webb, a.k.a. dread locks too long, and my lawyer, Mr. Logan Heatherton Esquire, and his awesome partners at McNees, Wallace and Nurick.

If I forgot anyone, it was not intended, but thank you.

Introduction

Since elementary school, and amongst many new era people of this land, a peculiar story of the finding of this land is taught, retold, analyzed, and dramatized. The story of Christopher Columbus, Pocahontas, slavery and many historic First Nations Peoples. It's a part of America and is speculated to one day wake up those having American dreams and show them a happy and peaceful reality.

"Remember, in order to know where we are going, we must respect and understand that from which we came."

My wishes are that the readers research the vast history of this land and understand that, if they were born here, you too are indigenous to this land, and this land had a name, a culture, and an identity way before it was labeled America. And it still does.

But this book dives deep into a dark and untold story.
State Correctional Institution Benner
Bellefonte, Pennsylvania
April 2019
R.R. Banks
The lives of Native Americans in the American prison system.

Preface

Our Ancestors are proud.

The things they knew long ago, and the messages they send now.

This book is a composition on a broadly shared and practiced Native American belief. This book is my visions, dreams and messages from the world of the spirits, who would like the world to know that they are very much alive. And that, in this current time, we shall see the hidden and forgotten truths. Many of our Native American Ancestors prophesized a rebirth of the First Nations People, and were accepting of the deaths they face. I am hoping that readers understand that the history of the Indian is very voluminous, and many of the Ancestors and Relatives died for the simple fact that they were Indian. Readers, please understand that the Native People have come a long way, and I am proud to say many of the Natives are strong, the teachings are still here, the languages, many are still being spoken and are still being taught. But also, many tribes are struggling and a systemic attempt at further genocide amongst us is still in play by the U.S. Government. Trust me, I know. I wrote this book as an incarcerated Native inmate, who is told daily I am only allowed to pray on Mondays. So, remember, there is still much work to be done. Our Ancestors informed us that there would be.

R.R. Banks
April 2019

Contents

From the Creator 1

The Drum Beat Within 6

I Am Free 10

The Birth of a Warrior 14

Action 19

The Battle of the Wolves 24

Pennsylvania is Not a Free State 28

The Truth Revealed 33

The Target 38

The Visit 42

The Ancestors are Indeed Proud 46

Never Forget 51

OUR ANCESTORS ARE PROUD

Chapter One
From the Creator

"The ground on which we stand on is sacred ground. It is the dust and blood of our Ancestors."
-Chief Plenty Coups, 1909

I once cried that my life sucked and I could never do anything right and that my life wasn't fair. Raised up in low-income housing in ghetto after ghetto, exposed and vulnerable to anything this world within a world had to throw at me, I never would have imagined that I had it so easy.

My story is not so different from the average kid growing up in the hood. Single mom, strung out on drugs, and not caring what she did to get them, while three helpless kids were left to fend for themselves. Best believe I had to grow up fast.

There weren't any father figures in my story either, so I had to learn how to be a man from the streets, or sometimes, if I got lucky enough to spend some time with an uncle that wasn't in jail, and my uncles were all gangsters that basically like jail. So, they spent little time with me.

I've seen the drugs, I've seen the violence from the neighborhood gangs who were willing to die over some colors and a ragged little, trash-filled, block. When I was there, I had seen a lot. But I have to admit, now that I'm in prison, I see that world I lived in in a whole new perspective. I also even understand it. I understand how I've ended up here, in this cell. And that the little world I was so familiar with was only a little piece of a very big whole.

Once I realized this, I realized how little I knew. I began to realize that I lacked knowledge of the world, and even further, I lacked knowledge of myself. I began to ask myself, who am I? I actually became enveloped in that question. There was not a minute in my day where I wasn't trying to answer this question. I even started asking other people who they were, just so I could see how they would answer. Now I must ask you: Who are you?

One night, in this cell, that very question became very clear to me. As I was sleeping, I dreamed back to this time when my grandmother told me that I was Indian.

She told me, "Marvin, my mother, your great-grandmother, was a Blackfoot Indian. That's where we got our good hair from."

No sooner did this scene replay itself in my dream did I begin to know myself. At the time, I must say that dream was strangely magical, but I did not know what I know now. I was given a message that night, and for the longest time, I didn't know it. I know this to be true, because my grandmother is still alive. So why would that old scene present itself to me in a dream?

There is only one logical explanation. The Creator wanted me to have this. My life has done a complete 360 since that night. I've read many books on my tribe. I've learned about the language. I've even begun to advocate for Native American rights. The Creator has made it clear to me how important it is for me to educate myself and to acknowledge his existence which I couldn't continue to deny any further.

For the longest, I was not a spiritual or religious person. I just didn't believe in anything and didn't care to believe in anything. My grandma would kill me if she knew that though! She loved her gospel, and growing up in her household, I didn't have any say so in the church matter. She made sure I read the Bible and was dressed to impress for service on Sundays. But, for some reason, Christianity just wasn't for me.

In prison is where I truly found religion. The prison has a

Native American service that I joined, and I must say, coming from where I've been, this spiritual path I've been led to is the best thing I've ever experienced. The connection was automatic and it felt so right.

I remember the first day getting called for service. I woke up that morning with butterflies in my stomach, I was so nervous. I had some strange thoughts going through my mind. I hope no one get offended, but I kept thinking that they were going to eat me or try to kill mee, because I was more black than Indian. I really was thinking this, man.

I was surprised when I got there. Everybody was friendly and kind. All of the brothers at the service just seemed so peaceful considering our crazy prison environment. The Native American service was a chaos free world of its own. I was still a little nervous, because I didn't know what to do, and I tried to step away and just watch, but they weren't hearing that for one of the first times in my life I had committed to something.

This is how the service happened as soon as I entered the chapel. A couple of the Native brothers came up with their left hands extended, not the right hand. The left for a greeting. So, I'm thinking, OK, a left-handed hand shake, that's new. As soon as I extended my hand to attempt to grasp the first brother's hand, he grabs my forearm and pulls me in for a hug. Can you imagine how I felt my first time doing this? Words just can't explain that one.

So that was the greeting. I did this about thirty times, with a majority of the Native brothers, saying things in languages I never heard before, while all I could fathom to utter was a simple 'Hello' in English. The conductor of this service, and one of my first teachers, was Ms. Jennifer Hudson, who, amongst us Native American prisoners, stood out like a sore thumb.

My ignorance led me to think various obscure thoughts about this woman, like how was she an Indian when she looked white? What could she know? I even found myself having lustful thoughts about her. All those things changed very fast for me.

Ms. Hudson directed all of us to line up. At this moment, she had two of the Native brothers burn some herbs, in which, one by one, people would step up and begin to rub the smoke of the herbs onto themselves. Beforehand, a big circle of chairs was formed, and inside this circle of chairs was a smaller circle of chairs, with the biggest drum I have ever seen in the middle of it.

For my first day, I sure had a lot to take in and a lot to get used to. As the line of people progressed, one after the other, towards the burning herbs to purify themselves before entering the circle, it dawned on me that I didn't know how to do this. I started to panic a little. I turned around to ask the person behind me, but was given a stern look by the others. At this time, no one was permitted to be talking.

I later found out that this was a sacred Native American ceremony called 'Smudging' and this was a time where we prepared ourselves for prayers to come, but also was a form of prayer in itself. With everyone else concentrating on their prayers, I had no one available who could assist me on how I should perform this ceremony, so I did the only thing I could do at the moment: I played a little game of monkey-see-monkey-do. Whatever the few remaining brothers ahead of me did is what I would do. So, I watched them closely. My four eyes never worked so well in my life. I was able to observe every little detail. I watched every single movement that they made with their hands down to the order in which they did this.

Then, it was my turn. I stopped up to the burning bows of herbs with two things in my mind. First, I thought to myself I hope I don't breathe the smoke in and fall out. Secondly, I hoped nobody could see me sweating. I know it might sound strange, but this was exactly how it happened.

Stepping up to the burning herbs, I finally realized that there was a lot of smoke emanating from this bowl. Matter of fact, the whole chapel was filled with it, and the aroma was unlike any other smell I had ever experienced. I can't really say if it was a good smell or a bad smell, but it had a smell. I have to admit though, I remember for that whole day, and maybe even into the next day, I smelled like those same herbs. This I liked so much that I began to walk around with this smell clinging to me like I was wearing a badge of honor.

But, back at the herb line, I mimicked what I had seen the other guys do. The only difference was that I did it faster, because I just needed to get it over and done with. Armpits soaked with sweat, I made my way into the circle feeling as if I was alive, as if I just found the secrets to a realm of confidence and strength that someone purposely tried to keep hidden from me. That was the day I met the Creator, and the day he told me that, one day, I would awaken the world and begin to make the circle whole again.

Chapter Two
The Drum Beat Within

The elders teach babies in the womb that the first things that house us are darkness, water and the sound of our mother's heartbeat.

Our Ancestors have indeed paved the way for us. Enduring some of the cruelest defilements known to man. In their presumed absences, we very much so see that they are still alive. They live and still exist through the stories they left behind for us to tell, the ceremonies and songs that we still continue to perform and sing. The fact that we still continue to do these things that our Ancestors have taught us and have passed on to us allows for them to still be felt, heard and remembered for ever.

It is safe to say that, as long as we remember, honor and cherish who we are, they will live on forever. We will also live on forever, and our ways, traditions and customs will never die.

For hundreds of years and during the establishment of America and the United States, we have seen or heard how the new people from the east strategically and cunningly usurped our nations from our lands. With all that we've learned of the past, it is important to realize that, even to this day, we are still being systematically targeted. The Elders have foreseen the events to come long ago, and nowhere have our present-day Elders, who are our links to the Ancestors in the spirit world, ever spoke of a day in which the Indian will be able to stop fighting and can begin to rest.

OUR ANCESTORS ARE PROUD

As a modern-day Brave, and a warrior for the earth, I realize that there is much more work to be done and that living this Native American life of servitude, we must wake up from the state of slumber we have fallen into and become aware. I speak as only a vessel and the deliverer of these important messages. To all of my Native relations, hear me. Please take heed to these facts concerning our existence. It is time we tell the world "We Are Here." We are strong and we are a proud people. There is no better time than now for us to broadcast the beauty of our culture. With one voice and one heart, we must unite to eliminate assaults on our women. No more Native women shall have to encounter any form of intrusions on their bodies or persons, and for our women who have been tainted through non-consensual sexual trespass, we shall be their voices. It is our duty to place them upon our shoulders and show the world who she is as a human being and who she is to us.

We shall also be obligated to ensure that justice is served for our female relations. These scorned women are our mothers, daughters, nieces, and, more importantly, the sole providers of our future generations to come. Isn't this why our Ancestors willingly risked and gave up their lives? Isn't this good enough reason for us to rally together? I asked my Native people, have you forgotten the ways of old? Have you lost respect for yourself and the ways of old? Why? Many are the children of our thriving clans and nations who are finding who they are by observing the things that we do. We must show our children the harsh truths we face and physically and spiritually prepare them against the numerous temptations and evils running rampant among us. All these things we must do.

But always, there is more. I speak to you from behind prison walls, in a world that has no law, but merely the policy of subjugation. I am identified by a number, which is ND5137. Physically, I am a slave and am unfree. Have you thought of me? We are relatives, right? I am also your brother. The many Native American prisoners, who our tribes have forgotten, are also alive and are also fighting at your sides, but you, my fellow Natives, haven't acknowledged us. Am I as dead to you as many believe the Ancestors to be? Has modern day technology distracted you from the grandfather's teachings of compassion and respect?

The question we should really be asking ourselves is, when shall we wait until a law gets passed that, once again, deprives us of our rights? When should we liberate and take the proper precautions ahead of time to ensure our people's sovereignty rights? Shall we sit back in anticipation of the deaths of the last of our noble leaders and elders? Or shall we begin to train new leaders to take their places before it's too late? My brothers and sisters from every Indian Nation, remember, we have always been one and our mother is the same mother, and in the times of our tranquil silence, it is her heart we hear beating through every aspect of our environment always leading our own hearts so we'll remember to remain "harmonious." This is why many of our people acknowledge the traditions and stories about our sacred drums. This is why I encourage all the readers of this book to ask some of the elders and teachers about the drum and to dedicate some time into learning the songs that so with the sacred ceremonial drums that are also prayers.

Hopefully, after reading this, you will be interested in buying a sacred drum of your own and for your families and friends to share the beauty of that Mother Earth's heartbeat that resides within its medicine.

Let's stop procrastinating. It's time we act now. One night, I was sitting here in my cell, working on a painting, and right in the middle of it, a voice inside of me said, "You shall make a drum." This is no lie. I do not know what sparked this idea or message, but I felt it as it manifested that there was importance in doing this deed.

Unfinished painting and all, I stopped and began to form a plan on how I would construct this strange idea of a drum. Put yourself in my shoes. You're in prison, and have little to no access to materials that are accessible out in society. You don't just walk down the street and into a store, or go into the woods, fell a tree to use the stump, then load up the rifle to go hunting deer. In the prison world, you have to improvise a little.

After I stopped my bear painting, I spent the whole rest of that night into the next day racking my brain over how I was to do this. First, I sketched a design on a piece of paper, establishing size, shape, skeletal reinforcements, and a color scheme. I went through various ideas for material to be used to create the drum's formation and, at first, I opted for a toilet paper, paper mâché, type of body that I figured would have been fairly easy, but turned out to be an utter disaster.

I then resorted to plan b, which was to use cardboard, which is accessible to us inmates and proved to be way easier. For the next three days, I worked diligently, mostly doing my work at night. Many hours were spent on this task. Every night, before I started working on this drum, I made sure that I purified myself with sacred herbs and gave the utmost respect to what I was preparing to do, because the drum is that sacred no matter if it's made of cardboard, wood, etc. The finished product turned out to be what I categorized as a masterpiece.

Thick layers of cardboard, hardened with water and paint, reinforced with tape and mop head strings, with a painted handkerchief used to wrap it as my decorative hide, equipped with a sturdy handle for portability. This drum is light weight, portable, and can bang with the best of them.

Even now, it's been months since I made it, but I still marvel at its beauty. It's funny, if you would see me with it, you would think it was alive the way I treat it. I've made it a little stand up on my cell wall out of soap and pen tubes and a nice little drum stick made out of dried wet toilet paper. This drum is sacred and Mother Earth's heartbeat is indeed here, too.

Chapter Three
I Am Free

"The tipi is much better to live in. It's always clean, warm in winter, cool in summer, also easy to move."
-Chief Flying Hawk

Back when I first came to prison, I was trapped. I am able to identify now how trapped outside of myself I truly was. Being locked up has helped me to observe, analyze and digest things going on around me. For so long, I was that chess piece engaged in battle. I was only able to see what was happening right in front of me, depending on how I swiveled my head or rotated my body. But, in doing this, I was sure to always miss something that was happening in another perspective, and as we all can relate, usually when you miss something or can't pick up on something, when you do, if you do, it's too late. And, missing even the simplest of details can prove to be detrimental to our lives.

Being in prison, I have been removed from the board, but am now able to observe from the outside of the action. Now I am able to pick up on things that I couldn't see before and that I may not have seen if I weren't removed.

Believe it or not, I am now what you call 'outside of the box,' figuratively speaking. I am above the world, at the best bird's eye view ever, watching everything down to the smallest detail in the same society I was a participant in.

Being in prison, I now understand, was not the worst thing that has ever happened to me, but had turned out to be the best gift and educational experience that anyone who is trying to spiritually grow can receive. In many religions and spiritual practices, it is common that people would go off to a mountain top or a secluded place to receive a message or vision.

This imprisonment is my isolation and I have indeed received messages, visions and other forms of enlightenment. In a sense, I have sacrificed my freedom so that I could be reborn. The great spirit has shown me the truth behind the symbology of the circle.

As Natives, we are taught that the circle is sacred. Everything we know that exists operates in a cycle. We see the sun, moon and stars are all circle and rotate in an orbit in circles. We were taught that the seasons, from spring, summer, fall and winter, all work in an invisible circle. The teaching of the circle has really helped me in understanding the patterns, routines and systems of every situation I am put in or faced with.

I understand that many things have a system of operation which revolves in a circular pattern. So, to say, even the process of our coming into this world can be seen as a circular system. First, we are born, as a child continuously growing while we reach the stage of adolescence or teenager. From this stage, we learn many things about our next stage, adulthood, where we still continue to grow and further mature and proceed to the next phase of our lives: old age. And at this stage, we are full of the wisdom from the things we have learned throughout our lives, but remember, we are still learning at this stage of old age. This is a very sensitive stage I've seen, because most old folks are stubborn in that they have been alive to see more than we have seen. And it always leaves me awestruck that, yes, they teach us the many things that they have learned throughout their many, many years. But I am also able to teach the elders about new things that have developed, or are developing now.

But, to the readers, be warned. Many elders you must be patient with. Many of them do not take kindly to you trying to teach them something. Not all of them though. But many feel as though there's not too much that we can tell them that they don't already know or haven't already seen. I do have to admit, this gets very interesting, and in the end, no matter how much we are different in generational years, we understand that we need each other, so it is important that we give our elders the utmost respect as they prepare for the last stage in our life cycle: death.

In our Native ways, we are taught not to fear death, but to embrace it and prepare our death song for this sacred day. This day in which we journey off of our paths and onto the spirit path that leads us to our Creator. We are taught to honor and respect this stage, because our Ancestors before us have all experienced this, and they have taught us that in this spirit realm they are still walking and are very much alive even after their deaths.

Learning about this sacred cycle and the symbolic nature of the circle has helped me better understand my current predicament. I have been able to understand the system behind my imprisonment and, like I stated earlier, I am able to receive messages from the great spirit and the Ancestors. I have been able to spiritually connect to them and to get to know and understand them and also myself. I have been able to also understand the other many circles of this works and it's all because of my imprisonment.

I can firmly assert that, even though my incarceration was, and is, unfortunate, I am glad that it happened, because if not, I don't think I would have truly been able to feel so free. I no longer resent waking up to face another day restricted by my confinement. And I no longer walk around in anguish about what I did wrong to end up in here. I now look to each day with hope for more, knowing and education and have a deep and sincere look inside at myself.

I have prayed for those hurt by my past actions and understand now the innocent victims were actually in all reality basically my family, and should be respected as such. These people are connected to me, and we are one. Every living seen and unseen thing in this world is my relative. I no longer hate and try to hide my past. I accept it and understand that not going through these tests then would not have led me to the knowledge and understanding that I have today. I would not feel so alive and free as I do today. My relatives have taught me all of these things, and you also can experience this. You just listen to the silence.

That is where I meet them and that is where they wait for you. Mitakuye oyasih!

Chapter Four
The Birth of a Warrior

"Five weapons a warrior must have with him at all times: Integrity, character, honesty, morals, courage."
-Bear Warrior

It was a long ride from prison to prison, fresh out of the hole after doing ninety days segregation between SCI Grateford and Campbell, I mean, Camphill.

Once more, I was woken up early in the morning and rushed onto a bus to be transferred to my final destination, or home, as they call it. The ride was harsh, being handcuffed and shackled on a prison bus, with no cushions on the chairs and no heating system while it was under thirty degrees outside. That was a totally horrible experience that I wouldn't want anyone to experience.

But, besides the smells of the other inmate passenger's body odors, bad breath and gas, I enjoyed looking out of my window at how life on the outside world was still thriving, and how it was still lusciously beautiful.

I really understood and had a deeper respect for the earth and the scenery I saw during the ride. Many thoughts began to rush through my head and I realized how I had taken my life for granted for so many years. And how I really never looked at the world this way.

Facing this reality broke me down. The Creator showed me what I've done and what I've given up. And in that exact moment, I made up my mind to do whatever I could to have back what I had given up and also to respect every person and thing that was presented to my life from there on out. In that moment, I swore to not only stand up for myself, but to also stand up and show others how to enjoy this peaceful bliss.

At that moment, I became a warrior. Shortly later, the ride was over and a new world of adventure and also a new chapter of my life would be discovered. Upon entering this prison, my nerves were calm, my heart was empty from the worry that I used to possess from giving into a new environment and having to start over. To me, being at SCI Benner for some reason felt like it was something I should be looking forward to. I really believe the spirits were definitely with me at that moment, assuring me that everything would be fine. I don't know who was with me, but someone was there.

After being processed in, I carried my property boxes down a long-paved road through an electronically controlled sliding gate and onto my block. The one and only H Block.

As soon as I hit the block, I noticed that this wasn't your average block. It definitely wasn't like any of the blocks I was on in the other jail. I had seen inmates surrounding a TV, playing Nintendo Wii. This was very strange to me, because I had never heard of prisons having video games. I had seen the regular card players and stuff like that. But a peculiar observation and realization was that this was a special block, and a majority of the residents here suffered from some sort of mental illness.

For a while, I kept asking myself why they would put me on this block. I didn't belong here, I wasn't crazy. I could not understand it for a long time. I later understood that, maybe, I could help these people.

I was lucky though, that at first, I didn't see anyone that I knew. Then, out of nowhere, I heard my name being called. I began to look around. Standing in front of a cell calling me, was my boy Poppa. Poppa was also with me down in Camphill. We used to play basketball together. We even had a couple vicious battles on the chessboard. I can't lie, I still get emotional about some of those wins he has on me.

Message to the reader: If we ever meet some time in the future or something, please don't mention chess to me. You've been warned!

Things couldn't have worked out any better. The officer gave me a door card with my name, photo and inmate number on it, and informed me that the guy standing in front of the cell was my celly.

I was fortunate. There were a couple different scenarios to how this cell pairing could have ended up. Being on H Block, where the majority of the people were mentally ill, and some more severely than others, I, a guy with, and I quote, "a little anger problem," could have ended up in a cell with someone who talked to themselves all day. Or someone who was afraid of water and refused to take showers.

I really have to use my words wisely here, because I'm a strong supporter and advocate for mental health. But when you haven't seen the various levels and diagnoses that are associated with mental illness, it can be scary. And, for my first time, all I can really say about being on H Block so that you can understand is that this is a very unique place. I could go on and on about the many adventures of H Block, but I may need more pens.

Anyway, myself and Poppa wound up being cellies. Poppa was a short, five-foot-six, Puerto Rican guy about my age, twenty-six or twenty-seven, from Philadelphia. And one of the best cellies I have ever had. Poppa and I had a lot in common. We both were fast to anger and were what the C.O.s considered dangerous. But we helped each other.

For the whole last year that we were cellies, neither of us had gotten into a fight or even been written up for a cell restriction. "We were focused"!

Like myself, Poppa had a lot on his plate. He just had a kid and was upset that he could not be in her life. There were nights we cried together over this.

I would like the readers of this book to know that, yes, prison is punishment that most convicts and criminals deserve, but no man deserves to be secluded from his child's life, especially if his crime was not sick, bazaar or sinister.

During the time Poppa and myself were cellies, we gained nothing but the utmost respect for each other. We both were very sincere in our religious beliefs, me walking the Red Road, and him a Christian. Not once did we argue over our differences or try to push one another's beliefs on each other. Instead, we found a lot of commonalities about ways, and began to educate ourselves on the reasons that this seemed so.

Like myself, my celly was determined to learn and pursued any and all opportunities in the gaining of wisdom, knowledge and understanding. We both were very eager to grow. We began to now only examine our own religions, but also the many other religions in the world.

I would like to express that, if you believe that things happen for a reason, hopefully I can persuade you, or already have. I can honestly say now with the level of understanding that I have on life, that leading up to the moments of enlightenment with my celly, the great spirit and the Ancestors led me up to that moment. They were with us both, even though my cellmate was practicing the Christian way. They were there watching every step of the way, showing me that which was important for me to see and learn. All the while also leaving signs and slues to their presence.

As I write this book, they are here now, showing me images within my consciousness on what it is I should write. The Ancestors are guiding my hand and, through me, I hope their messages can be acknowledged, even if they are being sent through me.

They hope you honor their existence. They want you to carry the message. They want us to fight. Armed with the knowledge and wisdom given from the Ancestors, I began to see that what laid ahead was a little more than a fight, but indeed was a battle. All of my life, I had fought as a soldier directed by orders. Now, I was being chosen as a warrior and was shown that I would find many battles, but was few to choose the ones I would wage.

    Readers, I chose not to wage, I chose to defend. I chose to fight a battle that's worth dying for. I am a warrior who will die fighting for our Native People's rights. I have been reincarnated as a warrior who will fight the fight of my Ancestors.

Chapter Five
Action

"Would you like to save the world from the degradation and destruction it seems destined for? Then step away from the shallow mass movements and quietly go to work on your own self-awareness."
-Lao Tzu, Hua Hu Chong

My celly has long since been paroled. He is home, reunited with his loved ones and beautiful newborn daughter. May we all pray that he succeeds in all that he does.

For a while after my celly left, I became very sad. I pretty much felt like I was on my own in here. And the truth was, I was.

I would like to express though that this time to myself was indeed needed. And the great spirit used this time to further show me many things. With this alone time, I was able to plan, picture and execute my next steps. The great spirit had reawakened my motivation to create again.

With this along time, I started hand-weaving headbands and painting elaborate designs on them. I had begun to paint and draw all sorts of native portraits with ease. Doing this allowed me to create and establish a Native American presence on my block, where in which before I thought I was the only Native on the block.

One night, I brought a couple of dreamcatchers I made out into the block, along with some Native paintings, and was able to draw quite a crowd. Sitting in the dayroom table, wearing one of the headbands I made, a guy walked up inquiring about the artwork he was seeing. He was very interested in my work. This guy later became my first actual best friend.

Christopher Morris, also known as Sleepy Rabbit, is one of the coolest old southern dudes I've ever met. While we were sitting at the table talking, he flat out told me that he was a Georgia raised redneck with some Cherokee ancestry. And I have to admit, I respected him for his blunt honesty. I was able to relate to it, because one of the grandfather's teaching is honesty.

But as I said earlier, in bringing my artwork out, I began to raise awareness. It first started slow, then one day I looked up and it seemed like half the block was becoming native, or being reminded of who they truly were again.

I always acknowledge that fact that none of the happenings in this book weren't done on my own. The great spirit and the Ancestors were indeed the driving forces behind this overall gradual uplifting of Native American prisoners. I am their puppet. I am a portal in which they work through. I did not just wake up with the full knowledge and understanding of these tasks that, even to this day, I am engaged in.

It has taken me years even to begin to understand my position in all of this. And, as the days do on and new obstacles are presented, I still ask myself what does it mean, and what am I supposed to be learning from this new adventure. I realize how little and weak I truly am compared to the great spirit's incomprehensible strength.

I understand now how little we human beings are in relation to the universe. And to prove this, I have humbled myself drastically, submitting eagerly to the honoring and remembering of those who walked the Red Road before me and those who will come after me.

I know this to be true, because, one day, Sleepy Rabbit informed me that he was going to start going to the Native services again. He had already conversed with me how he had gone to the

Native services in the past, but doing so was difficult for him. He expressed how I had given him a new sense of direction, when before he was stagnant and lost unable to find his road at all.

To my brother and best friend, Sleepy Rabbit, I am honored to have been in your life and I am grateful for the joy you have brought to mine. I remember the laughter and also the tears we shared together. I am honored to have been able to provide you with a sense of self-confidence and bravery while we faced adversity from our oppressors. To the readers of this book, Sleepy Rabbit was so brave.

That even though here in this prison, there is a policy that says no mohawks allowed. Sleepy Rabbit became so prideful in his Native ancestry and with the status as a veteran who served as a United States Seabee.

One day, when we were cellies, he told me, "You know, River, I deserve to have a mohawk style haircut. Is the Muslims can wear big beards, and the Rastafarians can wear dreadlocks, I should be able to wear my warrior style haircut, such as a mohawk."

He then affirmed that this was what he would do. That night, armed with only a razor and a comb, he began to cut his hair. First, he performed an hour of meditation to seek permission to do this from the spirits. Receiving his confirmation, he began.

We understood that this deed he was performing was very serious and sensitive. Two hours later, and with a little help from me, his task was complete. And I must say, this hairstyle really fit his personality. From what I saw and witnessed him styling his hair in this manner was an even further awareness raiser within the jail. The good aspect that I observed was many other people began to become interested in the Native ways and customs, and his simple hair style possessed the powers of the universe.

I witnessed this man go from quiet, timid, suffering from PTSD, depression and anxiety, to standing and walking with the beauty of the mountains. I had personally seen the Ancestors also working inside of him. I saw change! Things were great for a while. We received many new people at the Native service and studies. A once non-existent community was being formed.

Then it happened. One day, while we were walking to chow, a lieutenant began to harass Sleepy Rabbit about his hair. The lieutenant stated the policy that said no mohawks were allowed, and that he was going to have to cut his hair. I spoke as the witness to this incident, for I was the only one with him. Sleepy Rabbit informed this correctional officer/lieutenant that he was a Native American and also a veteran, and had protected rights to wear his mohawk style hairdo.

The lieutenant's exact words were that he did not look like an Indian, he looked white, and further stated that he didn't care what he was, "You're getting it cut one way or the other." This lieutenant threatened him with hole time and asserted that he would personally make sure he lost his parole.

Without a chance to inform our chaplain of this, or being allowed a chance to be accommodated, Sleepy Rabbit was intimidated and bullied into cutting his hair. The same confidence, strength and pride that he had obtained from his sincere belief and commitment to the Native ways was stripped from him in that moment. He was, once again, reduced to the timid, quiet, depressed person he once was. And, worst of all, he also felt humiliated.

I would like to attempt to share the emotions that we harbored that night in our cell. Rabbit couldn't understand why he was treated so unfairly, and he, a veteran who put his life on the line for the sake of his country and those across the waters, couldn't understand how even some of the people he proudly protected and served for, and risked his life for, could disrespect him for professing the claiming his Native American identity.

This realization really beat him up. Night after night, I offered him prayers, words of advice and encouragement. It took weeks to lift him up, but I succeeded. My friend, Sleepy Rabbit, has since transformed to another jail to undergo his programs, and once he is done, he will be home.

Before we split, he made me a promise. He promised to tell

the brothers at his new jail about the things I had done here, and to remain humble and strong when faced with trials and tribulations. And I told him the things we swear or promise are inferior, for if the Creator wishes these things, so they shall be, but what we do know is the promise of all truths. My brother, there is much more work to be done. We must act now. That is our truth.

Chapter Six
The Battle of the Wolves

"Anger comes to us because we lost contact with God. When we keep in constant contact with God, there is no room to be angry."
-Swami Ramdas

There was once a man so defeated by anger that he attended to it more than his own son. It first started off as little bursts of agitation. But, as the days passed, the anger grew to devour his being. Because of this, the son was sent to live with his grandfather to ensure his safety.

Things were quite different with grandfather. He had many things to teach and the son was eager to learn. Things were great with grandfather, but the son, deep down inside, was very sad and worried about his father, whom he loved very much.

His grandfather, sensing something was terribly bothering the boy, asked, "What bothers you, child?"

The boy, with eyes full of tears, responded, "My father hates me, but I love him. He can't even bear the sight of me because I look like my mother. Maybe he thinks me being born is what killed her."

Grandfather said, "The reasons you cry are not as you believe. I have something to show you, come."

The grandfather led the son through a maze of trails, telling him to pay close attention and observe every key details of the nature around them. Finally making it through the maze of woodland trails, they arrived at a special place.

Standing on a very high hill at a cave overlooking a vast sea of green, grandfather said, "When I was young, my father brought me here also at times when my mind and heart were conflicted. I also have brought your father here at times when he was troubled. This story I have to tell you has been told by many of our fathers before us, and now it should be told to you.

"A long time ago, when the war between good and evil was first waged, a boy was born. This boy was considered very sacred. He grew to do great things, but he also did some very bad things. This boy was said to have two wolf spirits residing inside of him.

"From the time he could walk, he would destroy or ruin the many good things he created. The boy had many talents. It is said that it was he who would bring the buffalo herds during times of starvation. His skills as a hunter were remarkable. He was so good at bringing in the herds and killing them that he begun to overdo it, and over time, there were little to no buffalo left.

"His people had become very distraught over this and were tired of his destructive nature. They decided to banish him from the tribe.

"At this time, many people had died of starvation, including the boy's mother. So, with angered heart, the boy vanished, never to be seen again by people.

"The boy was so beaten by his sorrow and anguish that he began to grow weak. He began to starve himself to death in hopes to be forgiven by the hundreds of spirits who died by his doing.

"One night, while asleep in a cave, the boy had a dream. In his dream, the grandfathers spoke to him from the clouds, saying that there must be a balance in all things in order for life to be harmonious.

"While looking at the clouds, the boy was shown two wolves engaged in a great battle. These wolves were unlike any wolves he had ever seen in his life. They were massive and possessed the powers of the world. One was white and the other was black.

They both were great and the battle he watched appeared to be evenly matched, and a winner could not be foreseen.

"For an eternity, it seemed like he observed this battle. He began to understand that these two wolves were himself, and that this war had been going on inside of him for years. Watching these two wolves, he realized that the winner would only be the wolf he himself gave power to.

"The grandfathers had shown him, not only a dream, but himself. They showed him that his good could not exist without his bad, and vice versa. But his bad had outweighed his good, and that is the side he had fed. The grandfathers showed him how now the same wolf he fed had devoured his life, and it is said the boy's bones remain in this cage, forever trapped in this dream and forever asleep, dead. And if you look hard enough into this cave, you can sometimes see a dark, shadowy wolf inside."

I really wanted to share this story with you, because I am sure we have all felt the power of our anger, and more times than none have witness the outcome of situations we are faced with when we give in or give power to our angers. We have come to understand that anger is a necessity and is essential to the balancing of our lives. It's just a part of who we are.

Being in this prison setting, it is very easy to be driven to anger. Prison is the motherland of hate, pain, sorry and this best friend of ours named anger. I have to admit, anger is my biggest enemy. Yes, there were times anger helped me. But I can definitely say that it has hurt way more people in my life than any other emotion, like sadness. And I blame this on the lack of knowledge on what balance was.

For me, anger was so bad that, one, is had landed me in prison multiple times. And two, when I was finally seen by a psychologist, it was determined that I had a very extreme kind of bipolar called impulsive explosion disorder.

I would like to express the seriousness and importance that we educate and raise awareness on mental illness issues. I would like to say that I have become an advocate not only for the Native prisoners here, but for every one faced with mental illness, or as I like to call them, imbalances.

I strongly believe, with the right treatment, and through spiritual growth, it is possible to overcome mental illness. I've done strenuous research on particularly Native American people, and have seen how rapidly, from century to century, we have been affected mentally by our past and present generations.

It becomes obviously clear that assimilation and colonization has led to many unbalances among our people. Our culture has even been in some instances influenced by the ways of the American society, and when this happens, sad to say, this causes confusion, and we seem to be distracted from the strength of our Ancestor's teachings.

It is important that we ignore the lure of temptation that is disguised to look fun, easy or even better. Because, if it was indeed that, don't you think the Creator would have made these things essential for us?

Our Ancestors had predicted these things happening long ago. There are cave drawings and other Indian arts that predate the coming of our pale brothers. And, just like the prophecies or stories in the Bible, our stories and foresights adequately tell of a future world of evil and the destruction of Mother Earth.

It is important that we hold dear to who we are and that we help those who have wandered astray, reclaim their identities. It is important that we remember the teachings and ways of the old ones and apply them to our everyday lives. These things the Ancestors have seen, and now we are seeing to be true.

I play as a messenger, bringing forth these words from the mouths of our past relatives as I feel them vibrating through me. I bring forth the proofs declaring that Native culture is the strongest and truest way of life.

Yes, the world is my backyard, but these prisons have been my playground. This is where I've begun to understand my position in the scheme of all things. This is where the two wolves have begun to fight as a team instead of against each other.

Chapter Seven
Pennsylvania is Not a Free State

"We love quiet; we suffer the mouse to play; when the woods are rustled by the wind, we fear not."
-Indian Chief to the Governor of Pennsylvania, 1796

I've stumbled across information about Pennsylvania that has opened my eyes and has helped me understand why U.S. Native American prisoners are having problems being recognized. It seems that states that have Indian Affairs offices are able to receive adequate resources that are needed. Pennsylvania, unfortunately, doesn't have an accessible resource center that provides for the many unique needs that us Natives have. This is what we are lacking, and this is what we need.

The history on the establishment of Pennsylvania is an intriguing one that dates back to 1681 by William Penn, a Quaker who believed in religious freedom. William Penn was a fair man. He acknowledged the presence of Natives that occupied areas in Pennsylvania and made treaties and policies that protected their area from being encroached upon.

For a time, everything was peaceful between the Natives and the Pennsylvania colony. All of this began to change when he died, and his son was appointed as governor in his place. Things from then on were hard, because his son did not have the same outlook as his father.

As more and more settlers arrived here, they began to need

more and more of the land and, basically, found that there was no way to live in peace with the surrounding Native tribes. Altercations began to arise between settlers and Indians, where whites would encroach upon the sacred lands of the people and degrade it with the cutting of trees and mining and destroying of the land, and later with the building of train tracks and roads.

We can only imagine how this made our Native relations feel, and the animosity and troubles these things created. Eventually, with many skirmishes and the outnumbered and outpowered Indians facing eradication, in order to save themselves, women, children and elders were forced to move west, seeking refuge amongst larger and more powerful Indian tribes, like the Iroquois to the north.

There are historic records of multiple tribes living and traveling through Pennsylvania by the likes of one of the many well-known trails, like the most famous Appalachian trail. The truth though about Pennsylvania and the people who currently live here today is that the majority are non-Native, and if asked, could not tell you much about what a Native American was. Further, they would tell you that there aren't any Native peoples residing here today.

I have news for any individual who may think that. We are here in Pennsylvania. We lived here before any European settlers have, and we are not going anywhere. The sad thing about that statement, though, is that, because of risks of being discriminated against and ridiculed on the basis that an individual may be Native or of Native ancestry, many of the Native peoples are afraid to claim their heritage, and instead hide who they are from their neighbors, employers, and even friends, and it shouldn't have to be that way.

What did amaze me when I started doing research on Natives of Pennsylvania is that it was said in archeologists reports that indigenous people are found to have arrived in Pennsylvania 20,000 years ago. This shows how deep Native culture is embedded and connected to this land. I've also found that one of the first Indian boarding schools was here in Pennsylvania, in Charlsie, Pennsylvania.

What this means is that there was an element of discrimination and conversion right here in my back yard. Indian kids were being taken, and I emphasize the "taken", from their families and forced to learn European education. These Indian kids were forced to give up their own way of life, their language, their beliefs, and say to say, the Christian missionaries claim was what god wanted. A lot of our elders were told that our ceremonies were evil, and if they didn't stop, they would go to hell. This Charlsie boarding school was one of the first of its kind, but it was here in good old Pennsylvania.

There are many little towns and cities and streets that show the proofs of our Indian ancestors' presence in this state. Many counties even have Indian names, like the Susquehanna, Tahlequah and Erie.

One of the worst massacres involving the Indian people also took place here in Pennsylvania. Whenever you have time, look into the Conestoga Massacre, which took place in Lancaster, Pennsylvania. This city tries and tries to forget this event, but things like this never truly ever go away. Two-hundred-and-fifty plus years ago is long, but it is not long enough to forget that a so-called group of vigilantes slaughtered fourteen Conestoga Indians on December 27, 1763.

There are many unanswered questions regarding this incident. There were many promises to keep the Conestoga Indians safe, but for some "strange" reason, it didn't happen that way. No arrests were made after these brutal killings. And, to make it worse, in 1701 William Penn signed a document granting the Conestogas "the full and free privileges and immunities of English law." The treaty assured the Conestogas that they and the English, "shall forever be as one head and one heart, and live in true friendship and amity as one people."

I guarantee that the massacre of twenty unarmed Indians, including women and children, was anything but friendly. That happened all those years ago, and in a sense, it is happening here once again in a Pennsylvania state prison now in 2019. And no, I do not mean that Native prisoners are dying or being killed physically, but spiritually and mentally we were systematically being eradicated. As of now, we are basically told how to practice our religions by non-Indians who, when asked, couldn't even tell you one thing about Native customs or traditions. But these are the people that tell us how we are allowed to pray and also when we can pray.

I'll give you an example of one of the discussions I had with the prison's superintendent about the Natives not being able to adequately pray. One morning I met with Superintendent Dr. Robert Marsh and simply stated, "Sir, us Natives need our own personal prayer pipes, drums and accessibility to be able to light sage and other sacred herbs every day of the week, because now we are only allowed access to these things on Mondays, hopefully if our services don't get canceled for some strange reason."

He said, "Mr. Banks, all I can tell you is to put in a religious accommodation request and ask the people who deal with religion."

I responded by saying, "I already have submitted accommodation requests, and they were all denied."

And can you believe all he was able to tell me was that I had to do the best I could with what I had. Which was nothing. That simple conversation really woke up the beast in me. And I've been advocating for our rights since. There's not a second in the day that passes by that I do not think to myself how I can make life better for the Native American communities in these prisons. Even now, as I write these words, my mind is calculating and brainstorming ideas. I really don't think the average person can multitask on such a level. I'm kind of amazed at it myself.

But, on a deeper aspect, I'm amazed at how much I'm growing spiritually, because in situations where you are fighting or even standing up for your rights, it's so easy to lose control and turn a situation from bad to worse. And I have done that many times, so it's very important that you understand to have a since of humility, because you can't help the people if you keep getting in your own way.

Chapter Eight
The Truth Revealed

"No book can teach that which the Creator shows me every day. Life!"
-Running River Banks

Have you ever stared into the clouds and wondered how something so shapeless could hold such beauty and grace? And find yourself listening to the winds as they dance about the earth, alone in your own tranquility and bliss? You start to feel as if you're not alone at all. Somewhere close by and afar someone is there watching and waiting. Just watching and waiting.

I have deeply begun to understand that, even when we don't think we are being watched, we're indeed being watched. One thing about taking those first steps onto the road of spirituality, "The Red Road," is that, once you do this, you become connected to the many manifestations of the spirit world.

One day, while meditating in my cell, I had a vision where, as I was walking, I observed from my being a very bright and luminous light that seemed to come from within me. All around my body, this light surrounded me, but from my head this light projected straight up into the skies. And I became very uneasy about this, because I knew that this light would attract all types of attention. I didn't know from who, but I knew it would.

No sooner than I began to have these thoughts did my vision

become very "interesting." Things started to appear and even communicate to me, and I say "things" because I really have no words to describe what these things were. Maybe they were spirits, maybe something or even people from another world. I don't know, but I saw them and remembered them all this time.

My spiritual advisor, Chief Bailey, really helped me understand the concept or ideology behind this vision by stating every day and every moment of our lives should be lived as if our grandfathers and grandmothers before us are still out there watching us.

And it's strange, because there are times I'll be talking or joking around and I'll be overly aware and cautious about my choice in words. I've become scared to use profanity, or even have bad thoughts towards someone, because I feel as though the Ancestors don't just see me, but they also see my heart.

I picture it like this. It's hard to deal with my grandmother here in the physical world. So, imagine dealing with multiple grandmothers at the same time, who all have this great multitude of mysterious knowledge, understanding, and conscience. There are just some waters I wouldn't dare to tread in, and that's one of them.

But, by having thoughts like these, you will find yourself in a sense of daily practice and have a sense of remembering that I better watch the way I do things, because you really don't want to piss the wrong Ancestor off.

If anyone hasn't experienced interactions with the spirits, I would like to make you aware that some of them have the strangest of humors. So, just as we can irritate them, they also will, at times, cause quite the disturbance in our lives.

There have been times where I'll be stuffing my face with all kinds of snacks. Not thinking twice that I forgot to follow tradition and place an offering. I'd literally eat a bag of chips, then all of a sudden, I'll feel guilty for not placing a portion to the side to honor them first. Then, all of a sudden, I'll have pictures falling off the walls and even stuff like books and cosmetics knocked off the shelves.

And you just know when something like that happens, the first thought is that there was nothing strange about that. "Hey, that book just coincidentally fell." This majority of the time is not the case for me. The first couple of times, I thought this picture fell, okay, no biggy. The things on my shelf are moved around, maybe I did it and just didn't remember. Then there was this one day I came in from the yard and my mandala that I had affixed to the ceiling light was on the floor, approximately two and a half feet away from the light fixture, which automatically raised my suspicions. It still doesn't seem as though it is even possible for it to have landed so far away. That was one of those events where you had to be there in order to believe it.

Another strange events where I was able to actually feel the presence of our Ancestral spirits was on a Monday morning at Native services. On this particular day, Chief Good Bear, also known as "Chaplain Bailey", was conducting a healing ceremony with us in the chapel. There were about fifteen of us Native community members present this day. Everything in the day was just as ordinary as any other day. It was early morning, bright blue skies, early spring. Everybody was in high spirits, eager to begin the healing ceremony. This was actually my first time ever participating in a healing ceremony, so in al actuality, I wasn't too eager. I really didn't know what to expect.

We set up the chairs with the big "cancega" down in the middle, the sacred alter at the west, and our entrance to the east. We then all proceeded to our smudge purification ceremony where our two brothers, Brazil and Rambo, facilitated this wonderfully. After every one had smudged and entered the circle, all the while singing the spirit welcome song, we awaited Chief Bailey's emergence from his office to conclude the final smudge which completed our circle.

When he finally came out, I can say I did have an eerie feeling. I'm pretty sure the others felt it, too, and the only way to describe this feeling is by saying that it felt good.

Chief Bailey came in and got right to business. He instructed us all to lay on the flow on our backs with our eyes closed and pray. This we all did. He taught us how important our breathing would be to fulfilling our healing journeys. So, he informed us that we should all relax ourselves by inhaling four seconds of air and exhaling it for eight seconds.

As I began to do this, I, for some reason, became very uneasy, because, for me, I wasn't comfortable having my eyes closed around other people. Also, it was very hard for me to stop my thoughts from running. It was almost like, the longer I would lay there, the harder for me it was to stop more thoughts from rising.

The whole time I was going through this battle, Chief Bailey had begun to sing healing songs on the hand drum. And I must say that listening to the hand drum really made a difference in helping me relax. In all honesty, I felt like I was being hypnotized, as if I was slowly being guided into a deep sleep.

At this point, I had to be dreaming, because my conscious from somewhere within said to me, "It's dark in there." And wherever I so happened to be, did appear to be very dark. It wasn't a scary darkness, though. It was more like a mesmerizing darkness of the universe. It's like the pictures you see in books and magazines of the space pictures captured by satellites from NASA. You see this black void with the colorful smoke mists dancing around. That's kind of what I saw in my dream state.

At one point, I was in another world, looking at faces in a river, in which I felt like I was falling in to. No sooner did I begin to fall when I was abruptly awakened. It took a couple of seconds for me to realize what was going on. But, to my right, one of the brothers had entered a full-blown seizure. Everyone became extremely alarmed by this, and in a sense, panic kicked in. Chief Bailey was the only one who remained calm and was able to successfully bring this brother back to a steady conscious state.

By the time the medical team arrived, this brother was literally holding a full conversation with "Chap," which was amazing in itself, because the way his body was shaking against the ground, I thought it was the beginning of the apocalypse. You couldn't tell me that the whole earth wasn't shaking, and people's hands weren't popping off. I'll tell you this though: if he would have gotten up off the ground and started eating people, I'm sorry to say this, but it's him or me and I would've had to Walking Dead him.

All jokes aside, the whole experience was enlightening. I really grew to understand and respect the powers that the spirits possess. Chief Bailey explained it to us like this: He said, during the healing ceremony and before the seizure incident, he observed everybody, one after the other, twitch or move as the healing spirit visited us and once the spirits reached Brother D, he stated that the spirits stayed for quite some time, which means that this individual was in need of a lot of healing. He may have even, in a sense, possessed an evil host and the invisible battle that ensued between the positive healing spirits and this negative energy was too much for his body.

When he informed of us this, it made absolute sense. And I would like to share this with the readers of this book. I know that the knowledge of this situation is true, because I personally witnessed this individual's habit on a daily basis, and there was, indeed, major imbalances, along with spiritual and mental disturbances. I've witnessed that this individual was placed in the hole and has not been seen since. So, I would like to tell you that we can go through life second guessing ourselves all we want, but there will come a time that, if things are meant to be shown to us, we will see.

Chapter Nine
The Target

"Imagination is okay as long as you always remember and pursue the vision."
-Running River Banks

I remember how it all began. The mission that is. Angry that I had failed in life, and that I was back in prison with no one to blame but myself, I tried to put my imprisonment on everybody. I made excuses, like if my grandmother would have raised me better, I wouldn't be here. If I had known my dad and had a mom who cared, I would have had a better chance at success. I've tried every way to pass the blame, but, in all honesty, I am the blame. Me! And it took a very long time for me to accept that.

It all hit me the day Chaplain Mark Cassels sang the saddest song I have ever heard in my life. I'm talking, this song was sadder than any opera song I've ever heard. And I am a fan of opera music, by the way. Just don't ask me any titles or singers' names, because I don't know any, but I love the way it sounds.

The song he sang was even sadder than the Titanic theme song, which, in all honesty, broke me all the way down. It's been a couple of years and the day is kind of vague. All I remember is Chaplain Cassels mentioning that a very special elderly woman was very sick and might not live much longer. He then explained how important the elders are to communities and nations, because they are who teach us all the songs, ceremonies and traditions. He had said that it was very important that we learned everything the elders had to teach before they passed, so that the next generation could pass it on one day, keeping our ways alive.

After teaching us the lifecycle and the positions of the elders, he felt that we should all take a moment and honor them with a song prayer. With no hand drum or anything, he sang. It was like a scene in a movie, except it was real. Standing at six-foot-two, long brownish hair, and clean-shaven face, which made him look as if he were only about fifteen years old. He showed us what it was to be a native. He showed us how to connect with the universe and everything else in existence.

I couldn't understand the Lakota language that he was using for the song, but with this song you didn't need to understand what was being said, because you could feel it. I felt like he was telling all the spirits that are traveling to the spirit world that we would never forget them.

Please do not quote me on that, but that is how I felt. My eyes started to water and my throat began to squeeze. I tried to hold the tears back. This I just could not do and they fell anyway.

The song was so strong and powerful that even the Correctional Officers in the hallway came into the chapel and began listening in awe. Chaplain Cassels, if you ever read this, I want to truly thank you for that experience. I have been singing traditional songs since. I hope that one day I become as good as you.

That day I really think that, in a sense, I was reborn. If not that, a door was definitely opened for me. I began to think differently, and I had a sense of respect for everything: even the C.O.'s. Somewhere deep down inside, I felt and understood that we all possess those same powers to change, not only our surroundings, but our atmosphere. We have the power to create or destroy.

It became clear that the only way to right our pasts is by fighting for a better future. And fight is exactly what I began doing. Even as I write these words in this book, my mind is hoping that they call me down to receive legal mail, because I am awaiting a response from the United States District Court, Middle District of Pennsylvania on my sweat lodge lawsuit.

If you would like to research this case, it's cited: *Marvin Banks v. Tracy Smith et al., civil number 3:19-CV-0427*. And, by the way, this lawsuit began was indeed motivated by the effects of that one sad song. Allow me to show you how this is so.

So, I got transferred to my home jail, SCI Benner, where I currently reside now. And, after weeks of observing the issues within the Native community here, and after already being previously motivated, I decided that I was going to solve and correct these problems. I then began to do research on Native American prisoner issues, in which, I was amazed to actually find that there were voluminous amounts of data gathering done already.

I observed that there was even legislation passed that provided stronger protections for us incarcerated Natives. The most popular statute being the Religious Freedom Restoration Act of 1993, which has a subordinate that specifically applies to state departments or agencies, titled the "Religious land use and institutionalized persons act." This act, in which the courts refer to as its shorter abbreviated name "RLUIPA", has become my best friend, and should become everyone's best friend if they ever run into a problem regarding their religion where an official or state entity interferes.

The sweat lodge, as of now, is only one out of seven suits that is underway. And it is going really well. The Department of Corrections basically denied my religious accommodation for no reason at all, being that there was once a sweat lodge here in Pennsylvania before that ran for many years with no problems.

The Department had claimed in its denial that there were concerns of security, safety and fiscal responsibility. But I have so far defeated the defendant's exaggerated claims.

This case, I'm hoping, should be over in the spring of 2020. I do not believe that all I have done is one big coincidence. My being able to receive legal documentation, which would help my mission, isn't something that just happens. In an esoteric way, I believe I was able to reach out and connect to the spirits, who in turn led me in the direction I was supposed to go in. Many people aided me in this adventure.

If Steve Rozniakowski would have never asked his mom to see what information she could find, I really do think my journey would have been twice as difficult.

But, with the many individuals who had leant a hand, including the Pennsylvania Prison Society, there has definitely been those who have attempted to sabotage all of my efforts. In this book, you will also be able to view come of the misconducts I received from officers where I did a pretty bit of hole time.

So, tell me, is it all a coincidence that I was able to be released from the hole and able to send motions to the court on time? I became the target and still willingly take on backlash from this Department and its employees so that none of my brothers and sisters in the future will have to endure what I and so many before have endured, so we could freely exercise our religion.

I am the target. If you need help, I've made it easy to find me. And to those who hate, I've painted a big red X on my back, so you can't miss me.

Chapter Ten
The Visit

"They'll come in the day. They'll even visit in the night. So, I tell you, run, but you can't hide."
-R.R. Banks

By the time she came, I was in a very deep need. Who would have thought that this little old lady would be sent all the way up to this prison for me? I had called on the spirits for help and they answered me.

Ms. Judy reminds me of one of those old ladies that sits home in front of the fire knitting, while a fresh batch of homemade cookies bake in the oven. Having a visit with her was a very humbling and warm experience for me.

Previous to this visit, I was seriously battling myself in trying to keep my composure. Deep inside of me, anger and hate were being planted. It was so bad that the anger and hate had successfully breached the door to my mind, which was, in turn, affecting my thought process.

I really struggled with this, because I'm one of those people who is uncomfortable with having something wrong and needing help. I had already seen about ten psychologists and about five psychiatrists, and every time I decided that I didn't need their help and that I would handle things my own way. And, if you are like me, I encourage you to take any and all help you can get, because, if you allow your ego and pride to get in the way of things, like your mental health, you could become a danger to not only yourself, but to others.

I have experienced both of these dangers firsthand. I would like the readers of this book to know that, not only have my mental illness led me to become harmful to others, I have also "attempted suicide." And this is a very sensitive topic for me, because I was always one of those tough guys who said I would never do that. That's a weak thing to do. But yet, I found myself restricting my own breathing with a sheet that was tied to a cell vent. In an attempt to, in my mind at the time, just end all of the pain.

I want to express the seriousness of this. Prison can be a traumatic experience or it can be an experience of enlightenment. But, with the way that these prisons are going, I personally see more people becoming traumatized by their prison experiences, because these prisons have lost sight of the objective of rehabilitation and now focus on ways to budget and make more money.

I know this to be true, because it is clearly seen when I expressed this to the prison the important that religion has played in the rehabilitation process for inmates since the establishing of prisons/penal systems on this continent by Europeans. From the very beginning, religion was the number one tool utilized.

When I had informed re-entry specialists and psych doctors of this, they are dumbfounded and lost on what to do next. Which shows there is definitely work to be done within these prisons. If this prison and the PA Department of Corrections did really care about rehabilitation, they would have looked into the ways sweat lodge ceremony has been utilized by non-Natives and Natives.

To aid drug and alcohol abuse treatment, along with its benefits in the aiding of physical and mental illnesses. If rehabilitation was indeed one of the Department of Corrections' mission objective, why would they neglect in at least trying to administer the sweat lodge as a tool? The answer seems to be because of two things the Department doesn't care about sweat lodge, because they aren't making any profits behind it. And secondly, they just really don't care about rehabilitation, especially for Native people.

So, hopefully, you can see by putting yourself in my shoes how easy it is to become angry at things that are going on around me, especially pertaining to the ability to practice my Native religion, traditions and customs.

Excuse me for getting carried away. Ms. Judy from Prison Society was my Wonder Woman who came and rescued me as I was holding on for dear life. She couldn't have come to visit me at a better time. We talked about a lot: me, her, the world and jail. We even talked about god.

Ms. Judy stood up for my cause of being able to practice my religion freely. She was so serious about this that she told me as soon as she hit the parking lot that she was going to make some phone calls about Native American issues. The whole experience gave me a spiritual and emotional boost. It really amazed me, because she is a Christian and believed deeply in the bible and God, and still she went out of her way for me, a Native American prisoner.

The Creator and the spirits really showed me the essence of life that day. I was in need of a message or a sign that would give me hope, and they sent it through her. That message was definitely received.

To the readers of this book, it is very important that you don't allow your own opinions and perceptions become illusions that hinder you from seeing the very little details in every situation and aspect of your life. Many of us have learned to treat every person, small to old, as if they were sacred. Even those you dislike. I now understand this teaching, because Ms. Judy just happens to be a Christian follower, and if I would have let my opinions get in the way, I could have easily missed the fine detailed message that was shown to me in this experience.

It was easy for me to say, she's this, I'm this, this ain't going to work. And it's easy for anyone of us to miss a teaching or a sign, so give it a try next time you're confronted or conversing with a stranger. Don't judge, listen, and pay attention, and most times you will find that you at least learned one thing from the situation, whether it is something about that person or yourself. But I guarantee you will learn something.

Chapter Eleven
The Ancestors are Indeed Proud

"Just like the vision that black elk had where it was up to him to fix the broken circle so the saved tree could live. I am doing. My mission is not complete, but the Ancestors assured me that I will do it."
-R.R. Banks

It took me three times reading Black Elk Speaks before I was able to grasp the spiritual and esoteric meaning behind the vision he once had. In his vision, he talked of a broken circle or hoop, which I now understand to be his nation of people. Also, in his vision, he speaks of a tree that grows in the middle of this circle, but because of the circle being broken, the tree had died and the people were becoming sick and hungry.

In his vision, the seven grandfathers gave him the knowledge and power to save his people. I believe that also with me. I was shown the broken circle and this circle just happens to take on many forms and aspects of life. It can be the circle of emotions and thoughts within you. It can even be the environments around us, from the home to the world abroad.

It is for us to distinguish the faulty circle from one that is in wholeness. Once this is done, we become the initial tree. Before prison, my life was definitely a broken circle, sad to say. Even though I kept busy every day, even at times I thought my life was perfect, it wasn't, because everything I was doing, I was only doing to fill a void with the accumulation of money and materialistic binge shopping. But still, in my life, I felt I was missing something. This only led me to more suffering. I began to try and fill the void with relationships, which never seemed to be enough.

This led me to thinking that maybe I could forget about it for a while, so I started selling drugs and drinking, which only made the void worse. The void wasn't even filled when I found out that I had a daughter. So how is it that it has taken prison, the place that is considered to be the worst place in the world, to be the factor in my life that has removed the void? I must say, inside myself I don't feel that constant churning. "All is at peace!" My mind seems to be clear from the anger and cloudiness it used to possess. I have become wise and have learned to understand and have compassion for others. I give all things to the Creator great spirit for guiding me towards this Red Road way of life.

The read road way of life has done many things for me, and it can for you, too. It is said you get back only what you put into your walk. If you put forth good and productivity, that's what you will get back. If you put in bad, evil and corrupt things, that's also what you'll obtain. So, the choice if always yours.

I have been touched deeply by the ways in which my Ancestors lived and because of my commitment to these ways have they showed me the broken circle that I would have to fix. I will never say that these things are easy, but would like to express that there is always work to be done. Even when you get done on duty, you should be ready to jump right back into action. The Red Road is a way of life that requires each and every one of us to be of service to the people and majority of the time sacrificing yourself. In turn, this leads to beauty and the building of strong communities (circles) where in the middle of all this beauty and growth you'll see life.

I must imply further that the tree of life or peace must definitely be planted and shown proper care and attention in order for the circle to be strong. I sit here now, and I asked myself it is a coincidence that I have always had a deep infatuation with the stories about the tree of life? So much that, years ago, at age eighteen and nineteen, I would get a tree tattooed on the left side of my face. I've been told to have this tattoo removed, and my grandmother was also highly upset when she saw it, but yet it is still here.

I have indeed planted a seed that is growing by the day. In me fixing the broken circle of U.S. Native prisoners incarcerated here in Pennsylvania and those who struggle to be able to practice our traditional ways and customs while imprisoned. I encourage to be patient and "hold on!" The tree is growing and, just last week, the judge from the United States District Court for the Middle District of Pennsylvania granted my motion for appointment of counsel stating that my sweat lodge lawsuit has merit.

With that good news, you can almost see the Ancestors smiling and dancing in joy over this. I would like for the readers to interact with me and share their thoughts on what you think the outcome of this sweat lodge lawsuit will be. Do you believe the spirits are working behind the scenes to make this possible? I want you, the many readers of this book, to follow this adventure so you can see for yourselves how this plays out. I want you to observe how a forgotten nation becomes a forgotten nation no more.

Contact me at:
Marvin Bank
#ND5137
SCI Benner TWP
P.O. Box 33028
St. Petersburg, FL 33733

OUR ANCESTORS ARE PROUD

R.I.P.
Dennis Banks
And thanks to all the greats who've made it possible for us to connect with these sacred traditional ways.

Never Forget
By Running River

I was taught to pledge allegiance to the flag, and that Christopher "Columbus" found this land. I was taught that god gave his only begotten son to perils of his own creation, so he could die for our sins. I was taught how to speak with proper pronunciation. And that when I turned 18, I'd be free from my parents and in your society would now be considered a man. These things I've learned and may never forget. You gave me these tools or, as you have called them, gifts, but in these things that you've taught there are a couple things that you have missed. You never did tell me that I was different from you. All you've ever taught me was how I should be like you. You never did tell me you had secrets to tell. Or how I'd never succeed because I was programmed by you to fail. You never did tell me what happened to all the others my peers. Who were just like me, but showed you no care. Instead, I was told those who survived and I must be honest, the stories that they've told me expose all of your lies. They've taught me who they are and explained how we've become. They showed me that I was worth more just like them and also to never be ashamed, I've learned to respect all of existence and to live for others no matter how different or religion. I've learned that I am one of them. I am not like you and never will I be. But my people's ways are strangely secret and mysterious to you. And shall always remain uncivilized to you. But to us they are beautiful and meant to be cherished, meant to be learned and taught to future generations. I have been taught and educated by both a world of tyranny and also by a world of peace and beauty and am now ready to raise my people from their slumber so we can finally look you in the eye. Not as aliens, but as equals. As humans who deserve respect and will forgive but never forget.

RUNNING RIVER BANKS

OUR ANCESTORS ARE PROUD

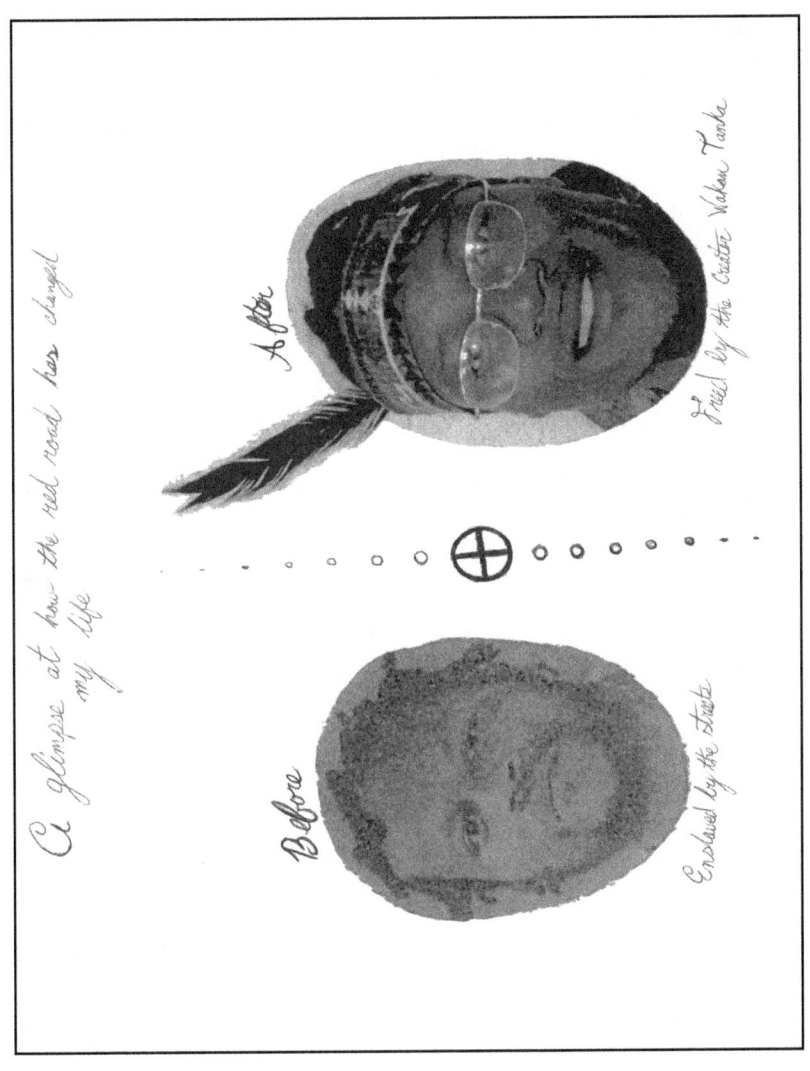

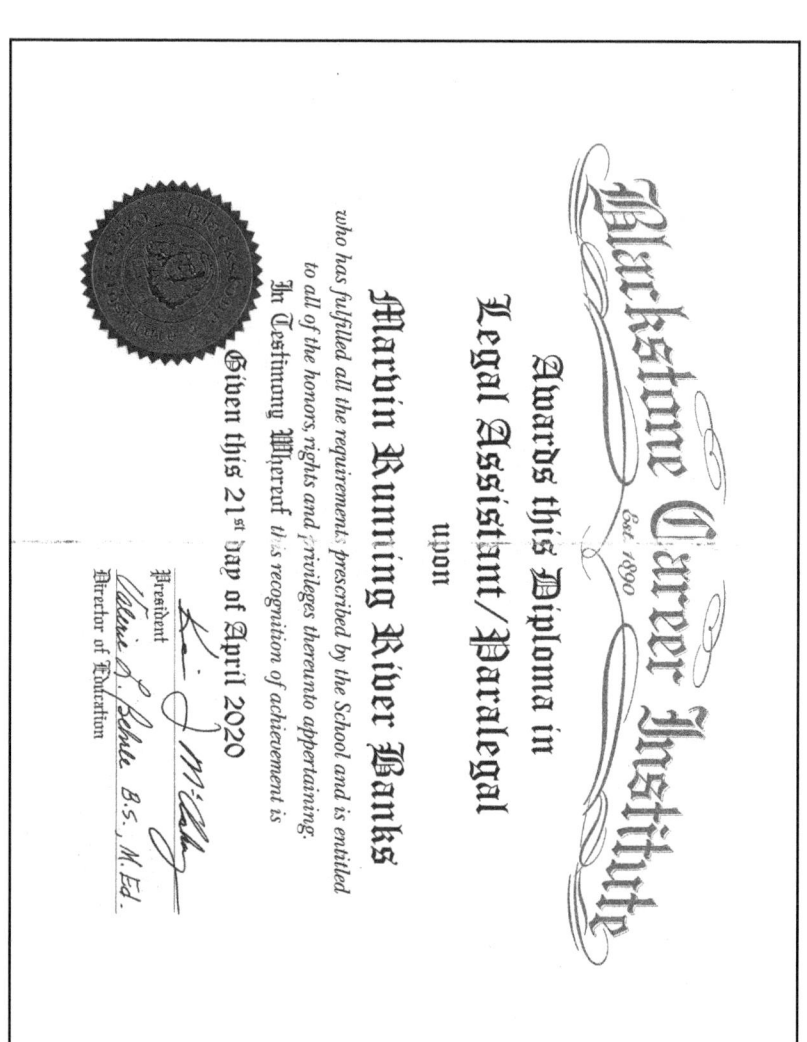

OUR ANCESTORS ARE PROUD

RUNNING RIVER BANKS

OUR ANCESTORS ARE PROUD

RUNNING RIVER BANKS

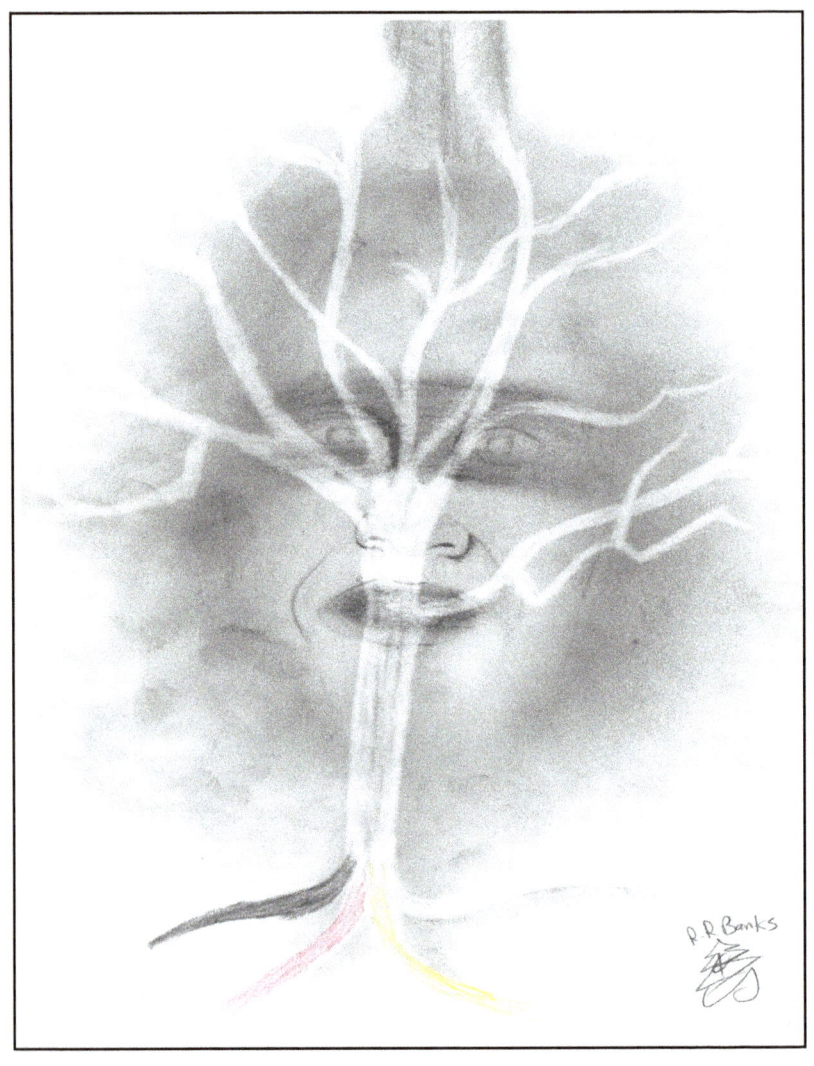

OUR ANCESTORS ARE PROUD

100 Pine Street • PO Box 1166 • Harrisburg, PA 17108-1166
Tel: 717.232.8000 • Fax: 717.237.5300

Logan Hetherington
Direct Dial: 717.237.5201
Fax: 717.237.5300
lhetherington@mcneeslaw.com

January 14, 2020

VIA OVERNIGHT MAIL

Special Mail: Open Only in Presence of Inmate

Marvin Banks/ND5137
301 Institution Drive
Bellefonte, PA 16823

RE: Amended Complaint and Scope of Representation

Dear Mr. Banks:

    Please find a copy of a draft Amended Complaint regarding the civil lawsuit captioned *Banks v. Smith et al.* pending at docket number 3:19-cv-00427-ARC-PT in the U.S. District Court for the Middle District of Pennsylvania (the "Civil Action"). Please carefully review the Amended Complaint and confirm the truth of the allegations contained therein. As a reminder, we will have an opportunity to discuss the Amended Complaint via a telephone conference on January 16, 2020, at 10 a.m.

    As we previously discussed, this letter also delineates our understanding as to the scope of our representation provided to you in the Civil Action. Our engagement is limited to representing you as to your religious accommodation request for a sweat lodge. Accordingly, the claims set forth in the Amended Complaint are limited to the sweat lodge issue.

    While we are aware that you may have other claims relating to the practice of your religion and accommodation requests, we make no comment on the merits of those potential claims and likewise are not representing you in regard to those claims. Note that the Amended Complaint may make reference to certain facts with regard to those claims for strategic reasons; however, the inclusion of those factual allegations in no way constitutes an agreement on our part to represent you as to other claims except for that of the sweat lodge religious accommodation request.

    Additionally, the materials that you have provided to us which relate to potential claims and/or issues other than the sweat lodge denial will be returned to you in a separate mailing.

www.McNeesLaw.com

Harrisburg, PA • Lancaster, PA • Scranton, PA • State College, PA • Columbus, OH • Frederick, MD • Washington, DC

www.ingramcontent.com/pod-product-compliance
Ingram Content Group UK Ltd.
Pitfield, Milton Keynes, MK11 3LW, UK
UKHW061222180426
11947UKWH00026B/1962